W9-ASN-970

★ *GREAT SPORTS TEAMS* ★

THE DETROIT

HOCKEY TEAM

Tim O'Shei

Enslow Publishers, Inc.

40 Industrial Road	PO Box 38
Box 398	Aldershot
Berkeley Heights, NJ 07922	Hants GU12 6BP
USA	UK

http://www.enslow.com

To the fifth grade classes of 1999 and 2000:
Memories are treasures.

Library of Congress Cataloging-in-Publication Data

O'Shei, Tim.
    The Detroit Red Wings hockey team / Tim O'Shei
        p. cm. — (Great sports teams)
    Includes bibliographical references (p. 43) and index.
    Summary: Surveys the key personalities and games in the history of the
Detroit Red Wings hockey team, winners of the Stanley Cup in both 1997
and 1998.
    ISBN 0-7660-1282-4
    1. Detroit Red Wings (Hockey team)—History—Juvenile literature.
[1. Detroit Red Wings (Hockey team)—History. 2. Hockey—History.]
I. Title. II. Series.
GV848.D47 O85   2000
796.962'64'0977434—dc21   JAN 1 5 2001   99-053163

Printed in the United States of America

10 9 8 7 6 5 4 3 2 1

To Our Readers: All Internet addresses in this book were active and appropriate
when we went to press. Any comments or suggestions can be sent by e-mail to
Comments@enslow.com or to the address on the back cover.

Illustration Credits: AP / Wide World Photos.

Cover Illustration: AP / Wide World Photos.

Cover Description: Steve Yzerman holding the Stanley Cup.

CONTENTS

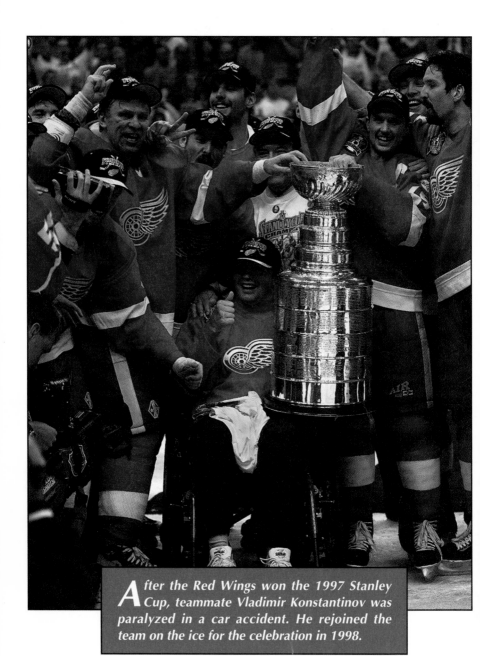

*A*fter the Red Wings won the 1997 Stanley Cup, teammate Vladimir Konstantinov was paralyzed in a car accident. He rejoined the team on the ice for the celebration in 1998.

BELIEVE IN DESTINY

Four, three, two, one—Bzzzzzzz!!! BELIEVE! Never has a buzzer sounded so magically musical. To the Detroit Red Wings, this final-seconds countdown on the evening of June 16, 1998, signaled the end of their season and the delivery of their second straight Stanley Cup. More important, it allowed their teammate to join them once again. After one year away, Vladimir Konstantinov was back on the ice.

Twelve months earlier, the defenseman's body—and his career—had been crushed in a limousine accident. The wreck came six days after the Red Wings had won their first Stanley Cup in forty-two years. The players were partying and, as the team encouraged them to do, were getting rides in limousines rather than driving themselves. But the limo driver lost control of the car that held Konstantinov, defenseman Slava Fetisov, and team masseur Sergei Mnatsakanov.

The car crossed a median and crashed head-on into a tree. Konstantinov suffered head injuries, Mnatsakanov was partially paralyzed, and Fetisov's injuries were relatively minor.

For five weeks, Konstantinov lay in a coma. As the entire Red Wings franchise prayed for Konstantinov and Mnatsakanov, everyone realized two things: First, the Stanley Cup brings little joy when your friends are nearly killed. Second, they had to win it again. They had to bring the Cup back to Detroit.

Believe

That was the Red Wings' mission throughout the 1997–98 season. The team's motto was "Believe," as in "Believe that we can win the Cup." Throughout the season the Wings wore a "Believe" patch on their jerseys. They battled injuries, rivalries, and contract squabbles all season, finishing second in the Western Conference.

The playoffs were no easier. In the quarterfinals, Detroit faced Phoenix in a series that seemed to be a cinch for the Wings. Instead, the Coyotes pushed the series to six games before the Red Wings won. The same thing happened when the Red Wings played St. Louis in the semifinals. In the 1999 Western Conference Finals against powerhouse Dallas, the Stars and Wings clashed in a tight series that featured skilled scoring and gifted goaltending. Detroit beat Dallas in six games, scoring 13 goals against the Stars' 11 in the series.

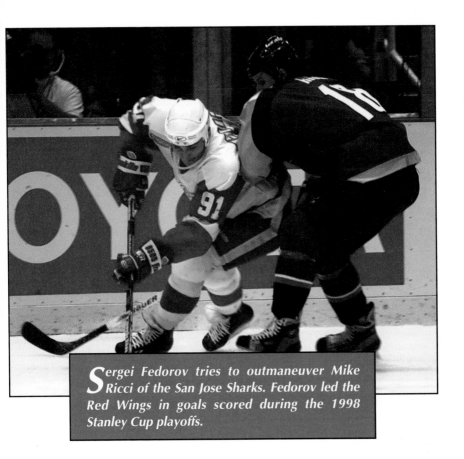

Sergei Fedorov tries to outmaneuver Mike Ricci of the San Jose Sharks. Fedorov led the Red Wings in goals scored during the 1998 Stanley Cup playoffs.

That brought the Red Wings back to their favorite stage: the Stanley Cup Championship Series. This year's opponent was the Washington Capitals, a team seeking its first-ever Stanley Cup. Compared to Detroit's roster of famous faces, Washington had few stars. The Red Wings knew how to win championship games; the Capitals had not played in many big games. Detroit won the first three games of the series by scores of 2–1, 5–4, and 2–1.

With the Cup just one win away, Detroit's coaches reminded the players of their ultimate goal: "Believe."

Somebody wrote these words on the locker room wall: "Faith is to believe what you don't yet see; the reward for this faith is to see what you believe."[1]

Vladi's Back

"Before the last game our coaches mentioned to us that they would trade anything for the win," said superstar forward Sergei Fedorov. "We felt the same way but, in words, the coaching staff put it together for us."[2]

And the team put everything together that night at the MCI Center in Washington, D.C. With Konstantinov watching from his wheelchair in the stands (Mnatsakanov was unable to make the trip), the Red Wings cruised to a convincing 4–1 victory. As the clock ticked to zero, goalie Chris Osgood heaved his gloves and stick high toward the ceiling, lifting his hands in celebration. The rest of the team followed, cradling the Stanley Cup on the ice.

Soon, the players' cheers turned to tears—but these were tears of joy. Konstantinov, still in his wheelchair, was back on the ice. All season, his locker back in Detroit had remained untouched, his equipment still hanging. They knew he would never use it again, but it reminded them to believe.

Having Vladi back now was unbelievable. His teammates placed the Stanley Cup in his lap and wheeled him around the ice. Some bent down and, in a voice just loud enough for Vladi to hear, sang the Queen rock song "We Are the Champions."

*G*oaltender Chris Osgood played all four games of the 1998 Stanley Cup Finals against the Washington Capitals. He is shown here making a save during Game 4.

"It was a great accomplishment for our team to be able to win back-to-back championships," teammate Steve Yzerman said. "It was a real thrill for us. We were really happy Vladi was there. It would have been perfect if he was there in uniform."[3]

They say nothing is perfect, but how much closer can you get?

*T*he home fans give Red Wings defenseman Paul Coffey a standing ovation after becoming the first defenseman to record 1,000 assists for his career.

The Detroit Red Wings and the team's fans proudly call their city Hockeytown. Few teams in professional sports have as many dedicated fans and championship trophies as the Red Wings. The vision of one powerful person got the momentum started.

Seven decades ago, Charles Hughes believed that Detroit could become a "hockey town." A former sportswriter, Hughes loved competition and knew hockey was an exciting game to watch. Having worked for President Teddy Roosevelt, Hughes knew some important people, and as a businessman, he was wealthy and powerful. He used his influence to put together a group of investors. They spent $100,000 to purchase an expansion franchise, the Detroit Cougars, from the National Hockey League (NHL) in 1926.

No Roar for Hockey

When hockey came to Detroit, America was in the middle of a time now known as the Roaring Twenties. People all across the land enjoyed dancing to the Charleston, spending money on fancy clothes and food, and tuning in to the radio to hear about the feats of America's greatest athlete, Babe Ruth.

The 1920s were a roaring decade, but the start of hockey in North America earned barely a yawn from sports fans. Hockey was known only as a strange, exotic game played up north in Canada, where ponds were supposedly frozen year-round. The first crowds drawn to the Detroit Cougars games were mostly Canadian. In fact, the Cougars played across the Detroit River in Windsor, Ontario, for their first season because there was no rink available in Detroit. John McManis, a sportswriter for the *Detroit News* wrote, "The crowds came to cheer for Canadian teams that played here and the support of the home rooters was almost nonexistent."[1]

That first season was hardly successful: a 12–28–4 record earned the Cougars a last-place finish, and the distinction of being the worst team in the league.

Help was needed, quickly and badly. The team was moving from Canada to Detroit's new Olympia Stadium, but the future of hockey in Michigan looked bad. It took a sharp hockey man like Jack Adams to help turn things around.

In 1927, Hughes hired Adams to be the team's coach and general manager, and though he eventually turned the franchise into a hockey powerhouse, things

The Detroit Red Wings Hockey Team

did not turn around quickly. The home game crowds were still largely Canadian, and those fans kept rooting against the Cougars. The team, meanwhile, continued to struggle, posting only one winning record (19–16–9 in 1928–29) in its first four seasons.

A nickname change from Cougars to Falcons in 1930 did not help much; the team still struggled and lost money. By the fall of 1933, the ownership group headed by Hughes could not pay its loans, so the bank seized control of the hockey club. That November, Chicago businessman James Norris bought the team.

The Winged Wheelers

A hockey fan who grew up playing the game in Montreal, Norris had earned his fortune in the grain business. Now he had a hockey team of his own, and he renamed it the Red Wings. For Norris, the name and the team's wheel logo were fitting. As an amateur hockey player, he had played on a team known as the Montreal Winged Wheelers that used the same logo. Also, Detroit was the home of Henry Ford and was the world's automobile empire.

Maybe it is a coincidence—or maybe not—but in that 1933–34 season, the Detroit Winged Wheelers skated to their first-ever first place finish. Still coached by Adams, the team made it all the way to the Stanley Cup Finals, losing to the Chicago Blackhawks.

Though that season ended sourly, it was the start of a winning tradition. The Wings would win their first

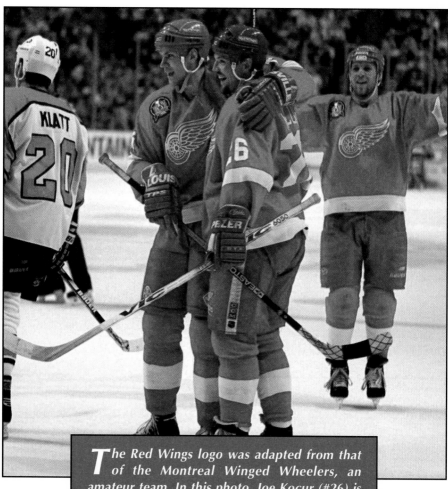

*T*he Red Wings logo was adapted from that of the Montreal Winged Wheelers, an amateur team. In this photo, Joe Kocur (#26) is congratulated after scoring a goal.

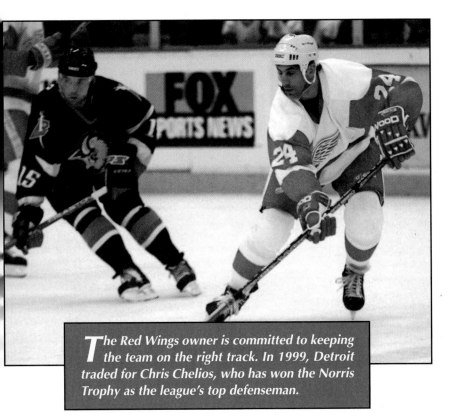

The Red Wings owner is committed to keeping the team on the right track. In 1999, Detroit traded for Chris Chelios, who has won the Norris Trophy as the league's top defenseman.

two Stanley Cups in 1936 and 1937—the beginnings of a dynasty.

Today, the team plays in downtown's Joe Louis Arena (where it moved in 1979) and is owned by Mike Ilitch, who purchased it from the Norris family in 1982. The setting and management are different from those early days, but the same goal remains: winning.

*G*ordie Howe is known as Mr. Hockey. At one time, Howe held the NHL records for games played, goals, assists, and points scored in a career.

REVERED RED WINGS

A walk through the back hallways of Joe Louis Arena reminds every visitor just how many superstars have played in Detroit. The walls are painted top to bottom with lists of yearly NHL award-winners and championship teams.

The hall leading to the locker room is decorated with bronze plaques of some of the greatest Red Wings. Forty-six Detroiters made it into the Hockey Hall of Fame in the club's first seventy-two years. From that group, a few emerge as the greatest players the game has ever known.

Gordie Howe, Right Wing

The hockey career of "Mr. Hockey," Gordie Howe, spanned nearly three wars, eight American presidents, 1,767 NHL games, and 801 goals. Slim but strong, Howe was perhaps the smoothest and most powerful player ever. Below his long neck, his muscular shoulders looked like two huge mountain slopes. Connected to his shoulders was a pair of long arms that could shoot a puck almost as fast from the left as from the right. Extremely durable, Howe was fifty-one when he played his last NHL season with the Hartford Whalers.

In the eyes of most people, Gordie Howe was the Detroit Red Wings. "There are four strong teams in this league and two weak ones," Toronto Maple Leafs star Dave Keon once said. "The weak ones are Boston and New York and the strong ones are Toronto, Chicago, Montreal, and Gordie Howe."[1]

Ted Lindsay, Left Wing

Ted Lindsay's complexion was rippled with scars from sticks, pucks, and punches—the battle wounds of a rough-edged hockey superstar. Lindsay was one of the NHL's most feared players, and not only because he scored 379 goals in his career. "Terrible Ted" was a remarkable fighter who thought nothing of losing a little blood to defend his team.

A member of the point-producing "Production Line" (Lindsay, Howe, and center Sid Abel), Lindsay was the also the Red Wings' locker room leader before he was traded to Chicago in 1957. Lindsay retired in 1960 but made a comeback in 1964–65 to help the Red Wings advance to the Stanley Cup semifinals.

Alex Delvecchio, Center/Left Wing

Alex Delvecchio often had a cigar clenched between his teeth, and his round face earned him the nickname

*T*ed Lindsay (left), Gordie Howe (center), and Alex Delvecchio (right) were three of the most dynamic scorers in Red Wings history. All three are members of the Hockey Hall of Fame.

Fats. Come game time, smoke would seem to rise from Delvecchio's skates as he danced across the rink; he scored 456 goals and recorded 825 assists in his career.

Gordie Howe once jokingly complained about playing on the same line as Delvecchio: "He is such a smooth skater with that almost delicate toe dancing style of his that he is worth watching. I can only watch him when he is playing on a different line than I am."[2]

Terry Sawchuk, Goalie

Terry Sawchuk was the perfect goalie: tough and gritty. Early in his professional career, a high stick knifed Sawchuk's right eyeball. At first, doctors

*S*ince the mid-1980s, Detroit has built its franchise around Steve Yzerman. Yzerman has not disappointed, captaining the Wings to two Stanley Cups in the 1990s.

thought he would lose the eye. Eventually, they sewed up the eyeball with three stitches, and Sawchuk was back playing two weeks later.

A goalie's game was vicious and violent, but Sawchuk lasted fourteen seasons with Detroit and seven more with other teams. Three decades later, he remained the Wings' best, having won 352 games for Detroit, along with 85 shutouts. The second closest, Harry Lumley, won 163 games and recorded 26 shutouts.

Sawchuk's career was spectacular, but his life ended tragically and suddenly. He died at age forty after suffering severe injuries in a non-hockey fight.

Steve Yzerman, Center

"Stevie Y" joined the Red Wings at age eighteen; he was team captain at twenty-one. Yzerman's best statistical years—six straight seasons with 100-plus points—came in the mid-1980s and early 1990s. As the team began winning in the mid 1990s, Yzerman's other talents, such as blocking shots and winning face-offs, were noticed. "As he's gotten older, I personally think he's gotten better," said Mike Ramsey, a former defenseman who played with Yzerman for two seasons and against him for many more. "That's just one man's opinion. I feel he's the best two-way player in the game."[3]

*T*he 1936 Stanley Cup champion Detroit Red Wings team picture. Jack Adams is in the front row, fourth from the left.

BENCHSIDE LEADERS

When Jack Adams was interviewed for the job of coach and general manager of the Detroit Hockey Club in 1927, he had a simple message for team owner Charles Hughes: "You need me more than I need you."[1] Hughes agreed; Adams was hired.

Jack Adams

For the next fifty-seven years, the Red Wings were his team. Adams was the man who signed and dealt players. Even after he gave the coaching job to Tommy Ivan in 1947, Adams kept total control over the Red Wings' roster.

A razor-tongued man who was known to throw orange peels around the dressing room, Adams was unmercifully honest. If a player was performing badly, Adams let him know. In his breast pocket he even carried train tickets to Indianapolis—where Detroit's farm club was—to remind players that they could be sent to the minors at any time.

Still, Adams cared deeply for his athletes, making sure the Red Wings had the best possible uniforms, equipment, medical care, and travel conditions. He hung a sign outside the locker room: "We supply everything but the guts."[2]

James Norris, Sr., the Money Man

Standing behind Adams was the man who signed the checks. James Norris, Sr., earned his fortune in the grain business, but owning the Detroit Red Wings was what really made his life rich. Norris, nicknamed Pops, loved hockey so dearly that he constructed a rink in the backyard of his home. (One of the job requirements for his butlers and chauffeurs was to play on the private hockey team.) Norris saved Detroit hockey by purchasing the club in November 1933, and though he left most of the day-to-day decisions to Adams, he kept himself involved.

Norris would fly from Chicago to Detroit on game days; after the game, he would board his private plane and fly home to Chicago. He would give Adams suggestions on player moves. For example, on February 14, 1941, Norris was concerned that if one of his goalies got hurt, there needed to be another player available. So he sent Adams a telegram stating:

LEAVING ON NOON PLANE. PLEASE MEET US AIRPORT STOP. SUGGEST YOU PUT TWO MORE GOALIES ON RED WINGS LIST TODAY . . . JAMES NORRIS.[3]

When Norris could not attend a game, it was always Adams's duty to call him directly afterward. (Norris even had a phone line installed on his yacht so he could get immediate updates.) "The toughest part of this job is to call Pops after a game and tell him we've lost," Adams said. "He just doesn't like losing."[4]

Fame from the Bench: Ivan and Bowman

The Red Wings' two best coaches have something in common. Both had hoped to be great players but suffered career-ending injuries, so they became legends from the bench.

First came Tommy Ivan, who began his professional career as a scout for Adams. When he took over the coaching job in 1947, Ivan led Detroit to six consecutive Stanley Cup Finals appearances, including three championships. In 1954, Ivan left Detroit and accepted the Chicago Blackhawks' general manager/coach position.

Scotty Bowman, who became a coach after fracturing his skull as a young player, arrived four decades later. In twenty-one seasons of coaching in St. Louis, Montreal, Buffalo, and Pittsburgh, Bowman had won six Stanley Cups. Who could better lead Detroit back to the top? Bowman's Red Wings won two Cups in his first five years.

Though his style is often mysterious—Bowman makes unpopular trades and benches star players—one thing is certain: He is one of the best coaches in sports history. He always seems to be thinking ahead of the opposing coach, almost as if he knows what the

*T*ommy Ivan (left) led the Red Wings to three Stanley Cup championships. With him are Bob Goldham (center), and Marty Pavelich (right).

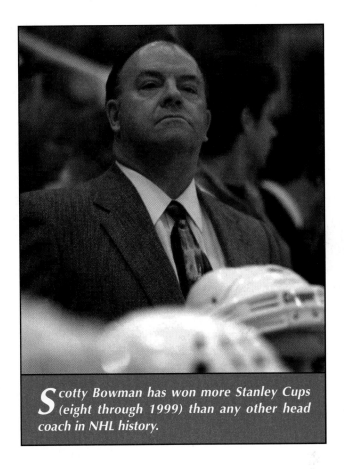

S cotty Bowman has won more Stanley Cups (eight through 1999) than any other head coach in NHL history.

other team is going to do before they actually do it. Bowman studies for each game like a college student cramming for an exam. His office at Joe Louis Arena is stacked three feet high with statistical packets, scouting reports, and media guides from around the league.

"I think he knows talent probably more than anybody in the game," says Mike Ramsey, who played for Bowman in Detroit, Buffalo, and Pittsburgh. "And I think his little quirks that he has, his little things, small things, details, make a difference in winning hockey games. He's definitely got his own style, but he wins."[5]

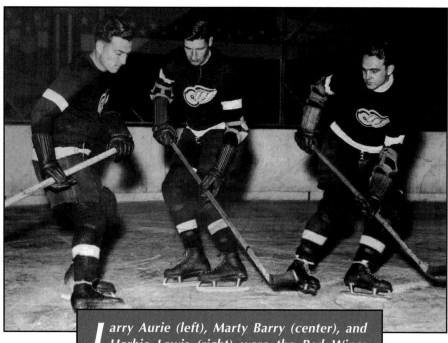

*L*arry Aurie (left), Marty Barry (center), and Herbie Lewis (right) were the Red Wings scoring line during the 1930s. In 1937, Aurie tied for the league lead in goals.

TO THE TOP AND BACK

I n the late 1990s, the Detroit Red Wings were the kings of hockey. But they have not always sat on the NHL's throne. During most of the 1970s and 1980s, the Red Wings were the jokers—not the royalty—of hockey. They missed the playoffs almost every year.

"It was awful," remembers Mike Modano, a Dallas Stars superstar who grew up in Detroit. "No one went to watch the Red Wings and no one cared, really, about what they were doing."[1]

But even during those garbage-dump decades, a shining past provided just a glimmer of chance for the Red Wings.

The First Cups

Under the coaching of Jack Adams, Detroit won their first two Stanley Cups in 1936 and 1937. The first Cup came in a best-of-five series against the Toronto Maple

Leafs, which the Wings won in four games. The next year, Detroit played the New York Rangers. The Wings won the series, three games to two, playing all but the first contest in Detroit. (After Game 1, the Rangers were not able to play in New York's Madison Square Garden because the circus had come to town.)

Detroit's stars in those years were center Marty Barry and right wing Larry Aurie, who were usually among the league leaders in points. Barry, who played in Detroit for four seasons, was one of hockey's first great playmakers. He led the team in assists for three seasons and is a member of the Hockey Hall of Fame.

The Dynasty

Another first-place finish in 1942–43 led to a third Stanley Cup for Adams and his boys, but the Red Wings dynasty did not form for another seven years. By then, Adams was the team's general manager only, while the coaching duties belonged to Tommy Ivan.

Between the 1948–49 and 1954–55 seasons, Detroit won seven straight regular-season titles. While Detroit's automobile industry thrived using assembly lines to make cars, the Red Wings flew with the "Production Line" (Lindsay, Abel, and Howe), which manufactured goals. Alex Delvecchio added more point-producing power. Imposing defenseman Red Kelly and gutsy goalie Terry Sawchuk guarded the net like a castle. Those supercharged teams had four superchampionship seasons.

The first came in 1950 against the Rangers. The final game in this best-of-seven series was locked in a 3–3 tie

The Detroit Red Wings Hockey Team

*T*erry Sawchuk was one of the greatest goalies in NHL history. He holds the all-time records for wins and shutouts.

and was not settled until the second overtime, when Detroit's Pete Babando scored to win the Cup.

Two years later, Detroit swept the Montreal Canadiens in four games to win another Cup. The Red Wings played Montreal again in 1954, but this series stretched to seven games. The Wings won in overtime again, on a goal by Tony Leswick.

If the Canadiens wanted revenge, they did not get it in 1955. Montreal and Detroit (then coached by Jimmy Skinner) again clashed in a seven-game series; the Wings won once more.

Finally, Montreal beat Detroit for the Cup, winning four games to one in 1956. It was the first of five

*B*rendan Shanahan throws his arms up in celebration after scoring a goal in Game 3 of the 1997 Stanley Cup Finals. Ron Hextall is the dejected goaltender.

straight Cups for Montreal; for Detroit, this series was the first in a long line of disappointments. The Red Wings would not win another Cup for over four decades.

___

Back in the Race

Finally, with stars like Steve Yzerman and Sergei Fedorov, the Red Wings returned to the top in the mid-1990s. Detroit made it to the Finals in 1995, but lost to the New Jersey Devils in four straight games. The next year, Detroit was eliminated in the conference finals, but they were not gone long.

By spring of 1997, the Detroit Red Wings were Scotty Bowman's team. It had been a couple of years since Bowman arrived in Detroit, and in that time he had hand-picked his players. Trading for forward Brendan Shanahan, defenseman Larry Murphy, and goalie Mike Vernon had provided the punch the Wings needed to make it back to the finals. "We are a team of destiny," said Sergei Fedorov.[2]

He was correct. The Red Wings crushed the Philadelphia Flyers in the championship series with a four-game sweep.

Their destiny seemed set, but when Vladimir Konstantinov was injured in the car crash one week later, the Red Wings' celebration ended. One year later, when they repeated their win and brought Vladi onto the ice, their destiny truly was fulfilled.

V yacheslav "Slava" Kozlov joined the Red Wings in the 1991–92 season. Since then, he has become an effective goal scorer.

OCTOPUS TALES

When a player scores three goals in a game, fans throw their hats onto the ice. When one team sweeps another in a playoff series, fans sometimes toss brooms over the boards.

Hats for hat tricks. Brooms for sweeps. In Detroit, they prefer another projectile.

The Octopus

In the past, when the Red Wings have played like champions, their fans have rewarded them by filling the ice with an ocean of octopi. Now that the NHL can call penalties against the home team when fans throw things into the rink, fewer octopi have occupied the ice at Joe Louis Arena. Still, the octopus remains an important symbol in Red Wings lore.

The octopus story dates back to spring 1952. The Red Wings were getting set to play the Toronto Maple

Leafs in the playoff semifinals. Jerry and Pete Cusimano were two brothers who ran a Detroit-area seafood store. They realized that if the Wings won eight straight games, the Stanley Cup would be theirs. A thought clicked: eight games. An octopus had eight legs. This would be good luck.

The Cusimano brothers brought the octopus to the game and threw it onto the ice. They were right about the luck. Not only did Detroit win that series in four games; they also swept Montreal to win the Cup.

For Wings fans, that was enough. Octopi brought good luck, so Detroit fans brought octopi to games. It is a tradition that always shocks new players who have never heard about the hurtling octopi, but they grow to love it.

"I'd heard about it a lot, but to actually get to see it once we started chasing the Stanley Cup, it's a really different feeling," says Sergei Fedorov, who came to Detroit in 1990. "Detroit stores have sold those things and they sold out. I guess it's neat, because it's a good symbol for this team. It relates to the road this organization has been through."[1]

An Original Favorite

As one of the NHL's "Original Six" teams—the others are Toronto, Boston, New York, Montreal, and Chicago—the Red Wings have enjoyed a popularity that has spread since those early days when they were booed in their own rink. Nowadays, Detroit players will see winged-wheel jerseys—and maybe even an octopus or two—in almost every city they visit. (But

The Detroit Red Wings Hockey Team

not Colorado: The Red Wings and Avalanche have one of the most bitter rivalries pro hockey has ever known.)

"The team has a tremendous following," says Steve Yzerman. "There are young people, and older people who followed the team through Gordie Howe, Ted Lindsay, Alex Delvecchio and those guys. When we go and play on the road, there are a lot of Red Wings fans."[2]

In the 1990s, Detroit became the most popular American hockey team in a former U.S. overseas rival—Russia. Some of the best Russian hockey players joined together to fuel the Wings' late-1990s championship drives.

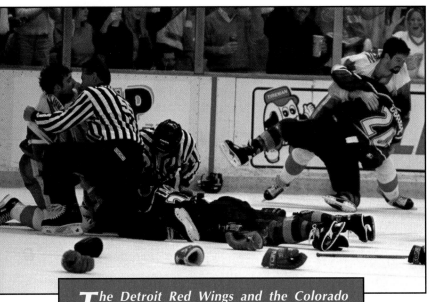

The Detroit Red Wings and the Colorado Avalanche are bitter rivals. Detroit's Martin Lapointe is being held back, while Brendan Shanahan scuffles over by the glass.

Niklas Lidstrom is one of the many talented Russian-born hockey players to have played for Detroit during the 1990s.

Russian Five

The group was led by the smooth-skating forward Fedorov, who slipped away from the Russian national team during a Seattle tournament in 1990. He surfaced in Detroit a few days later and quickly developed into hockey's brightest European star. Over the next few years, he was joined in Detroit by center Igor Larionov and defensemen Niklas Lidstrom, Vladimir Konstantinov, and Russian hockey legend Slava Fetisov. Together, they formed the formidable "Russian Five," a group whose national pride and skill was unmatched.

The quintet played together for just two years before that fateful limousine crash forced Konstantinov to retire. The Russian Five were gone, but their spirit stayed steady and spread throughout the team. The remaining Red Wings set out to win the Stanley Cup in honor of their fallen teammate.

"We knew that it was a very, very honorable and reasonable thing to do," Fedorov said, "and we tried our best."[3]

The Detroit Red Wings' best always brings one result: victory.

STATISTICS

The Red Wings History

SEASONS	W	L	T	PCT	STANLEY CUPS
1926–27 to 1929–30	64	87	25	.435	None
1930–31 to 1939–40	197	197	82	.500	1936, 1937
1940–41 to 1949–50	265	190	91	.569	1943, 1950
1950–51 to 1959–60	351	218	131	.595	1952, 1954, 1955
1960–61 to 1969–70	308	292	116	.511	None
1970–71 to 1979–80	267	410	115	.410	None
1980–81 to 1989–90	273	410	117	.414	None
1990–91 to 1998–99	390	226	88	.616	1997, 1998

W=Wins   **L**=Losses   **T**=Ties   **PCT**=Winning Percentage

The Red Wings Today

SEASON	W	L	T	PCT	COACH	DIVISION FINISH
1990–91	34	38	8	.475	Bryan Murray	3rd Norris
1991–92	43	25	12	.613	Bryan Murray	1st Norris
1992–93	47	28	9	.613	Bryan Murray	2nd Norris

ASON	W	L	T	PCT	COACH	DIVISION FINISH
93–94	46	30	8	.595	Scotty Bowman	1st Central
94–95	33	11	4	.729	Scotty Bowman	1st Central
95–96	62	13	7	.799	Scotty Bowman	1st Central
96–97	38	26	18	.573	Scotty Bowman	2nd Central
97–98	44	23	15	.628	Scotty Bowman	2nd Central
98–99	43	32	7	.567	Scotty Bowman	1st Central

tal History

W	L	T	PCT	STANLEY CUPS
2,115	2,030	765	.509	9

ampionship Head Coaches

COACH	REGULAR SEASON			POSTSEASON			STANLEY CUPS
	W	L	T	W	L	T	
ck Adams	413	390	161	52	52	1	1936, 1937, 1943
mmy Ivan	262	118	90	36	31	0	1950, 1952, 1954
nmy Skinner	123	79	46	14	12	0	1955
otty Bowman	266	135	59	63	33	0	1997, 1998

Great Skaters

PLAYER	SEASONS	YRS	GAMES	G	A	PTS
			CAREER STATISTICS			
Sid Abel[H]	1938–43 1945–52	14	613	189	283	472
Alex Delvecchio[H]	1950–74	24	1,549	456	825	1,281
Sergei Fedorov	1990–99	9	604	274	398	672
Gerard Gallant	1984–93	11	615	211	269	480
Gordie Howe*[H]	1946–71	26	1,767	801	1,049	1,850
Red Kelly[H]	1947–60	20	1,316	281	542	823
Reed Larson	1976–86	14	904	222	463	685
Nick Libett	1967–79**	14	982	237	268	505
Ted Lindsay[H]	1944–57 1964–65	17	1,068	379	472	851
John Ogrodnick	1979–87 1992–93	14	928	402	425	827
Norm Ullman*[H]	1955–68	20	1,410	490	739	1,229
Steve Yzerman	1983–99	16	1,178	592	891	1,483

* Does not include statistics from the World Hockey Association, WHA.
** Libbett played the 1975–76 season with Kansas City.
[H] Hall of Fame member

SEASONS=Seasons with Red Wings   **YRS**=Years in the NHL   **GAMES**=Games played
G=Goals   **A**=Assists   **PTS**=Points scored

Great Goalies

PLAYER	SEASONS	YRS	GAMES	MIN	GA	SH	GAA
			CAREER STATISTICS				
Roger Crozier	1963–70	14	518	28,566	1,446	30	3.04
Glenn Hall[H]	1952–57	18	906	53,464	2,239	84	2.51
Harry Lumley[H]	1943–50	16	804	48,097	2,210	71	2.76
Chris Osgood	1993–99	6	284	16,494	647	23	2.35
Terry Sawchuk[H]	1949–55 1957–64 1968–69	21	971	57,114	2,401	103	2.52

SEASONS=Seasons with Red Wings   **YRS**=Years in the NHL   **GAMES**=Games played
MIN=Minutes played   **GA**=Goals Against   **SH**=Shutouts
GAA=Goals Against Average

The Detroit Red Wings Hockey Team

CHAPTER NOTES

Chapter 1. Believe in Destiny
1. *Detroit News Staff*, "Game 4: They Said It," *The Detroit News*. June 16, 1998. <http://detnews.com/1998/wings/9806/16106170239.htm> (February 4, 2000).
2. Author interview with Sergei Fedorov, 1999.
3. Author interview with Steve Yzerman, 1999.

Chapter 2. History of Hockeytown
1. Jerry Green, "Detroit Bought a Winner, Then Built an Unforgettable Legacy," *Greatest Moments in Detroit Red Wings History* (Indianapolis, Ind.: N T C Contemporary Publishing Company, 1997), p. 7.

Chapter 3. Revered Red Wings
1. Peter Gzowski, "Great Gordie," *The Sunday Sun*, October 15, 1989; reprinted from the December 14, 1963, issue of Maclean's.
2. Pete Cuomo, "The Subtle Greatness that is Alex Delvecchio," *Hockey Illustrated*, p. 34. (Date unavailable; article in Hockey Hall of Fame Resource Center archives.)
3. Author interview with Mike Ramsey, 1999.

Chapter 4. Benchside Leaders
1. Jerry Green, "Detroit Bought a Winner, Then Built an Unforgettable Legacy," *Greatest Moments in Detroit Red Wings History* (Indianapolis, Ind.: N T C Contemporary Publishing Company, 1997), p. 12.
2. Phil Loranger, *If They Played Hockey in Heaven: The Jack Adams Story* (Grosse Pointe Farms, Mich.: Marjoguyhen Publishing Company, 1976), p. 250.
3. Western Union telegram dated "1941 FEB 14." Hockey Hall of Fame Resource Center archives.
4. Milt Dunnell, "He Hated to Leave if Wings Were Losing," *Toronto Daily Star*, December 5, 1952, p. 24.
5. Author interview with Mike Ramsey, 1999.

Chapter 5. To the Top and Back
1. Author interview with Mike Modano, 1999.
2. Cynthia Lambert, et. al, eds., "A Season Full of Magical Moments," *Quest for the Cup* (Chicago: Triumph Books, 1997), p. 20.

Chapter 6. Octopus Tales
1. Author interview with Sergei Fedorov, 1999.
2. Author interview with Steve Yzerman, 1999.
3. Author interview with Sergei Fedorov, 1999.

GLOSSARY

assist—The action of a player, usually a pass, that allows a teammate to score a goal.

center—Playing in the middle of the front line, the job of the center is to set up the wingers for shots.

defensemen—The players whose main job is to stop the opposing team's forwards from getting good shots on goal.

face-off—A method in which two opponents attempt to gain control of the puck, which is dropped by the referee.

forward—One of the three players that line up closest to the other team's goal. The forwards are also known as the right wing, the left wing, and the center.

general manager—The official in charge of the team's business and personnel matters.

goalie—The player whose main responsibility is to stay in front of the net and deflect away or block the opposing team's shots.

hat trick—Occurs when one player scores three or more goals in a game.

Hockey Hall of Fame—Located in Toronto, Canada, the Hockey Hall of Fame celebrates the history of hockey and the game's greatest players, coaches, and contributors.

lines—Arrangements of usually three forwards or two defensemen who go out on to the ice to play for shifts of roughly two minutes.

playmaker—A player who is known for his ability to set up teammates and record a lot of assists.

point—A player is given a point whenever that person scores a goal or records an assist.

Production Line—The Red Wings most famous line, featuring Hall of Famers Gordie Howe, Ted Lindsay, and Sid Abel.

puck—Black circular disk for playing hockey.

Russian Five—Group of five Red Wings players of Russian origin that played for the team in the mid- to late-1990s.

Stanley Cup—The trophy presented annually to the NHL's championship team.

sweep—When one team wins every game of a playoff series.

two-way player—A player that is known for both his offensive and defensive skills.

wing—The players that play to the left and right of the center on the forward line.

FURTHER READING

Bak, Richard. *The Detroit Red Wings: An Illustrated History.* Dallas, Tex.: Taylor Publishing, 1998.

Detroit News Staff. *Greatest Moments in Detroit Red Wings History.* Indianapolis, Ind.: N T C Contemporary Publishing Company, 1997.

Fischler, Stan I. *Motor City Muscle: Gordie Howe, Terry Sawchuk & the Championship Detroit Red Wings.* Toronto, Canada: Warwick Publishing, 1995.

Gave, Keith. *Red Wings' Silver Dreams.* Champaign, Ill.: Sports Publishing, 1993.

Greenland, Paul R. *Wings of Fire: The History of the Detroit Red Wings.* Rockford, Ill.: Turning Leaf Publications, 1997.

Detroit News Staff. *Quest for the Cup: The Detroit Red Wings' Unforgettable Journey to the 1997 Stanley Cup.* Chicago, Ill.: Triumph Books, 1997.

McFarlane, Brian. *The Red Wings: Brian McFarlane's Original Six, Vol. 4.* Don Mills, Ontario, Canada: Stoddart Publishing, 1999.

Podnieks, Andrew. *The Red Wings Book: The Most Complete Detroit Red Wings Fact Book Ever Published.* Toronto: E C W Press, 1996.

Rennie, Ross. *Detroit Red Wings.* Mankato, Minn.: The Creative Company, 1990.

Stevens, Jim. *Detroit Red Wings.* Edna, Minn.: ABDO Publishing Company, 1999.

INDEX

WHERE TO WRITE

Detroit Red Wings
Joe Louis Arena
600 Civic Center Drive
Detroit, MI 48226

WEB SITES

http://www.detroitredwings.com
http://www.nhl.com